LANSDOWN ANTHOLOGY 2010

LEAP ELECTRIC

Second edition 2010

Poetry Monthly Press

The Lansdown Poets

David Whitwell

David Graham Cook

Kay Baxter

Tim Burroughs

Geoffrey Ford

Mark Sayers

Rupert Hopkins

Mary Crowder

Charles Thompson

Olga Amelina Unwin

Contents

The Lansdown Poets

David Whitwell

David Whitwell enjoys the Lansdown group
and the stimulus it provides to keep writing.
He started writing poems in 2006 and likes
their modest ambition and the fact that they
get finished – unlike his growing pile of
unfinished novels.

Land Art

A mark on the ground is all it takes
to show I passed this way;
and sticks I pile in the wood,
in a simple wigwam shape
will last a few years
and perhaps someone will see
their slow decay.

The trees obscure brief works of man.
Imogen's camp[1] fades into leaf mould,
but if you go now,
there's still a trace of where they slept.

I wanted more;
something to remain after us.
A stone circle
hidden in the wilderness
might last a thousand years.
Such folly;
where will it end?

I will copy Richard Long[2]
my wandering landscape hero;
take a clear still day
and sit by the pond,
and with my finger
draw on the face of the water.
Draw an eye looking up at the sky.

[1]Imogen and friends built shelters in the wood and slept
there in summer 2004.
[2] Richard Long drew a crescent moon on the surface of Lake
Titicaca in 1972.

Kingfisher on the Roof

Kingfisher on the roof,
red sun behind palm trees
the whole sky on fire as
darkness falls,
6.30 prompt.

Chilled Kingfisher
eases the tropical night.
Buses and cars are honking
motorbikes buzz past.
And beyond, the trains,
real Indian trains, half a mile long,
all lit up, doors open,
people sitting on the steps.

No news today.
Nothing from home.
No papers, no BBC,
hard to recall recent events that seemed so important.

I thought of Lawrence on his Savage Pilgrimage,
travelling the world as a voluntary exile.
Was it this?
Escaping the reach of the old life.
He must have sat
in the golden hour
as the sun went down.
The true sun,
the one that has its back to us
and can't be seen from England.

And the message from my radio
– brought here to keep in touch...
not a whisper –
nothing from England
so the concerns from home
don't reach this far
and all that living-in-the-head-trying-to-sort-it-all-out
doesn't matter
up on the roof
with the Kingfisher
in the dark.

Thought I'd Know by Now

Thought there'd be an answer,
thought I'd know by now.
It always seemed a lifetime
would be long enough:
but time passes and nothing comes.

I've seen it in pictures,
figures in a landscape.
Old men in tatters
screwing their eyes against the light,
staring far off to the hills,
speaking in a language I don't understand.
And when it's translated
it's about djinns and devils,
people flying in the air,
speaking to the dead
and living for ever more.

I've chased it all my life;
so many false starts;
the hopeful glimpse, the headlong chase,
mysteries from the edge.
And I reel back, Is this it?
Is this all there is?
I might as well have stayed with the gypsy folk
wandering the green fields of old England;
or with Mme. Blavatsky dreaming up her crazy worlds
behind the veil. And there's a catch;

It's only for those with faith;
others need not apply.
And the words signify something else;
the secret that is always a secret;
that will never be revealed.
And if you think you have it:
if you grasp a little bit,
then you're wrong, it's somewhere else
and somewhere you can't follow.

All that is possible and I will never know;
but what if it is here and now;
and the only mystery is this.
This place in the evening light
with autumn coming on

and the voices of other people close at hand.

The Swallows of Jerez

That time we stayed with Justin,
the swallows were back in Jerez;
swooping over the houses,
calling out as they passed high in the air.

In the evenings we sat in Plaza Rivero.
Cool at last;
and we met Arve and his new wife
coming from their house in Calle Francos.

And we went to Seville,
and walked in the Alcazar.
But it's mainly the swallows I remember,
watching them on and on in the evenings,
swooping and skirling through the canyons of the old town.

Looking for T. E. Brown[1]

Books handed down from a man I never knew[2],
ignored and set aside for so long.
Never heard much; just 'he liked Conrad';
And 'could recite the dialect poems.'[3]

A sailor on a merchantman before the Great War,
He bought *Within the Tides*
In the English Bookshop
in Iquique in Northern Chile.

The poems, I spurned for years,
pompous, dated stuff.
Tried to shake them off
giving them away to Oxfam, to anyone
but somehow they stayed.

Then I was in Clifton,
Stuck there for years,
'Grinding at the mill';[4] just like him,
So I had to take them down,
And have another look.

He wrote of the island he loved but left;
Cultivating instead the nostalgia that
grows with time and distance;
familiar to the migrant's child.

So I sought him out,
Clifton's famous poet
in Redland Green Churchyard,
fighting through the brambles, growing thick as trees
round that neglected plot.

He's lost and forgotten now,
The Great Manx Poet.
So I sat in the sun and celebrated
that all things pass.

1: T.E. Brown (1830-1897) 'The Manx Poet'.

2: Norman Barlow - my Manx grandfather.

3: Brown was most famous for his poems in Manx dialect.

4: From 'Clifton', one of Brown's best known poems.

David Graham Cook

I feel that my scientific education failed me because no teacher helped me understand that Science would forever be the handmaiden of the Humanities. But Wittgenstein's remark, 'we feel that if all possible scientific questions are answered, the problems of life will still not have been touched at all,' fortified and inspired me. Some of these poems seek to suggest the limitations of Science without embracing the irrational.

Nothing Imagined

I

The words of the poet are beautiful,
flowers by the side of the road,
they have deepened the silence
were unguessed at:

where did they come from?

II

The words of the poet

where,

where did they come from?

And if they weren't here
would something else take their place?

No, nothing.

Nothing,
there'd be nothing imagined
and no gap where words needed to be.

The world's full:

full of chance and necessity,
heads or tails
heads and tails,

and   nothing   imagined.

Not Our Own

stark room
plain table
faces

with a flourish
steaming dishes
laughter

outside
the moon
behind cedars

beneath
children playing
in the dust

at a call
they scamper
indoors

Always the presence of the past
bright in flashing eyes
or a tone of voice

sometimes passion from nowhere
not thought of as innate
nor yet provoked.

How to find words for this scruple
over feelings
not our own nor yet another's,

should we say 'hint of a disjunct future'
or as further off than memory and sorrow
'trace of an earlier life.'

For surely we are marked by something different
dim within our darkness
but sensible nonetheless,

and if not yet
then tomorrow
or the day after.

Twilight Song

There is a world we did not build together,
a smile we did not share,
can I reach out and touch you?
No, you're not there.

That song, it's last chord sounding,
fades and we move away,
parting is heavy in me
and another day.

The dance between the light and shadow
has no other end than this,
heightened contrast, deeper brilliance,
absence twinned with bliss.

Cadenza

(for Sweet Chorus)

At a concert
an intricate sinuous phrase
triggers a shiver in my neck
which travels the length of my spine.

Delicious:
and a surprising reminder
of my distant ancestors
because for them the sensation
would have signified something different;
fear,
pleasure perhaps,
most probably just cold and damp.

It is both old,
and to come full circle,
as fresh as that musical shiver
with which Bird astonished New Yorkers
at Carnegie Hall
when he played the cadenza
right after the theme
of 'A Night in Tunisia.'

Note: 'full circle' because this poem remembers two concerts, one by Sweet Chorus in Churchill on 20th June 2009 and the other by Charlie Parker and Dizzy Gillespie in New York on 29th September 1947.

The Grammatical Web

If it is true that talk of reconciliation is absurd,
and here I assume that the future through us
shall determine the present and the past,
you will be right and I shall be wrong,
and as you have said and will be proved so justly to have said
'I can never give you what you want.'

My angry self keeps hearing this as
'I will never give you what you want'
not 'I am unable to give you what you want,'

but were I to try and establish a common sense
you could as well insist on the indeterminacy of translation,
so that perhaps in the end we should be forced to agree
that there is an inescapable obscurity
in the begetting of intention and capacity alike,
although the agreement would recapitulate disagreement

in the absence of any imaginable light.

Survivor

I turn back two pages
to look again at the photograph
of Marine Mark Ormrod
with Prince Harry and Prince William.
The photographer has taken the picture
from Mark's left side
so we cannot see he has lost his right arm
as well as both his legs,
the result of a landmine in Afghanistan.
Were I to meet Mark
I would find it difficult to be natural,
but alone am able to study the photograph
and try to understand my inadequacies and derelictions.
For I have not been tested like this
and feel guilty that Mark has had to suffer so much,
while with no particular merit
I have got through life
more or less unscathed.

Kay Baxter

Kay's life work has been a journey in healing springing from deep roots in the natural world, meditation, yoga and writing. She spends much of her time exploring inner and outer landscapes which feed herself and her work.

She feels working with poetry to be spirit food that brings a deeper connection to our feeling and which nourishes, sustains and soothes, particularly when we have been brushed by the harshness and imposition of the world with all its rush and push and so many man-made systems that drain and frustrate. In poetry she connects to a softness and a depth of being that touches like balm, bringing relaxation and a sense of renewed harmony.

Coming Home

Just sitting.
Window gazing
Breathing.
The song of the birds
flitting amidst branches
or perched atop the roof of the rough old stone wall;
outhouse and nesting place.
The jaw drops, relaxes,
softens my face,
and all around is soft too,
soft and spacious and quiet.
Cat upon my lap,
muffled hammerings of builders
building homes for other lives.
And me basking.
moments out of time
a gift to myself,
of allowing and giving fully
without hitches,
expectation,
conditions.
Demanding nothing of myself
a sweet being unfolds
is setting me free
as only the self can
to 'be'.
Being free is simple,
does not require any form,
money – things – other people,
it is essence itself
waiting for us to come home.

Note to myself

My wanting for joy and ease
To rain down upon me
has failed to notice
The joy and ease
That is right here
In every moment~
Born from a bright willingness
To receive each moment as it is
However it is
To rise and greet
Enthusiastically
With whatever is required.
It is a hesitant and tight resistance
That blocks and prevents~
Blinds dull eyes
To the sparkling light of possibility.
So rise up
Dispense with being defeated
Greet each challenge, problem, occasion,
Whatever presents,
Respond
Allow the river of yourself
To gather and flow
For whatever comes is what is needed
The grit for growth
Fuel to propel
Movement forward
On this crystal path.

Symphony of trees

As I write the wind moves gently
And the oak tree sheds her leaves
One in particular
A soft spiralling
Down past my window,
Catches me
Holds me still,
And now a shower of bronze sweeps
Following a gust,
Releasing those just ready, ripe
To be taken
And joyously it seems they go.
Wanting only to sit
Look past my window
Let go like the leaves.
Gazing now into the darkening day
The just there~ness,
Undemanding winter branches
Of the silver birch
Rising effortlessly up,
Wanting for nothing.

A Healing

Loneliness etched deep,
Seeps,
and envelops.
Once I would run from it
frightened,
into the company of others
the arms of lovers.
But now
when I feel it approach
I stride towards it
greet it,
Oh so warmly
for it is a part of me
'abandoned'
at the beginning of time,
small child
untended.
Now when she calls for me
I invite her in
eagerly catch hold of her unsure hand.
We play
bright simple games
or walk in silence giving thanks,
dancing together
we come close,
feel the joy in sorrow,
sorrow in joy
and it is all OK,
allowed, embraced, included.
Letting it all be
loneliness winds down
like soft summer rain
disappearing into
a fresh, new day
a day for skipping and swimming
for lying on hot grey rock
soaking sun.

Merging
we become one,
a rich and spacious whole
free at last.

Sweet honey

You are unique
and beautiful
Don't spoil yourself
In competition
In trying, striving
To be better than
More than
To outshine,
Overshadow
Another
This only diminishes
Your own glory.
Set yourself free
With the balm
Of co-operation
Where love meets love
A sweet honey
Spreading endlessly

Tim Burroughs

Tim has been writing poetry and enjoying the works of other poets since he was at school. His themes include travel locations that have awed him, inspiring musicians, artists, and dancers, love in the modern world, the sacred in a secular and commercial world, magic and mystery in a vacuum packed existence and the elusive emergence of poetry and song from the depths of the subconscious.

At Fjord's Edge

Blue-grey the sky
Green-grey the ground below
Light blue-white
The rolling tide

At fjord's edge
The world unfurls
Like clouds
Round granite peaks

Dawn rises slowly
Like cramped limbs at morning
Arms tired
Eyes straining to see the day

Life's quiet uncertainty
Rolls like the waves
Endless motion
The vagaries of fate
On a distant shore

the moment

the moment waits
disguised
as a dream
of yesterday

a pedlar
passes
with
a basketful
of cares

a shadowy porter
carries
the baggage
of the past
in a battered
suitcase

a stalk*
flies
overhead
dangling
the
crying form
of the future

the casket
of yesterday
passes
with
a jazzband
playing
'mood indigo'

a
key
shifts
sideways
on
a
black and white
pedestrian
crossing

a
blind
beggar
draws
the final
curtain
with
a
burnt
finger
of charcoal

*A 'stalk' is a vicious dark vulture-like bird that is best banished to the realm of the subconscious.

Sea Necklace

Nothing but the sound of sea on sand
The rhythmic slap of the waves
Beating on the shore
The pulse of the white moon
Overhead
Talking to the land
Bringing in the salt water
Gifts from the deep
Kelp, wrack and razorback
Natural beads
To fill the necklace of sea
Around the island
Linking land to the sky
The pulse of unity
Part of you and me

If I was to. . . would you?

If I was to hum a tune
would the melody reach out to you
would you hear the notes
drift through the morning air
would they mix
with the sound of the waves on the shore

would they echo in a cave
like a child's breath in a shell

would they course through your ear
to the heart of your soul
remind you of the one
whose love for you inspires this tune?

Geoffrey Ford

Geoffrey Ford practised, researched, expounded and taught librarianship from Hoo St Werburgh to Sydney, N.S.W., but has now retired. He has always been interested in systems and structures, and now enjoys the challenges of finding and fitting form to content in verse.

Marriage Lines

My wife's dad works on the railway,
My mother believes I married beneath my station.
My wife is blonde, with green eyes –
My mother suspects I was trapped.
When my mother visits, my wife weeps in the night.

I met my wife at university,
Our mums believe we are a perfect match.
Our son is a professor, our daughter's on TV –
Samantha Taylor; in Rome, for the Holiday Programme –
My wife and I take separate holidays.

My wife's family has a hyphen, they are old money,
My wife's mother believes her daughter married beneath her.
My mother-in-law suspects I seduced her daughter –
My wife has wide blue eyes.
When the child is born, I am having the DNA tests done.

School Run

It used to be mums –
Bright patterned dresses,
True English roses,
Black Pedigree prams,
Rocking new infants, gossiping gently.

Now it is dads,
Anxiously pacing,
Professional mothers,
Suited and booted,
Child seats and bull bars, no time to linger.

It used to be children –
Smock frocks and Alice bands,
Snake belts and short pants,
Crayons and loo rolls,
Hop, skip and jumping, the whole mile home.

Now it is kids –
Brand names and trainers,
Miniature adults,
Knapsacks and mobiles,
Belted in tightly, the slow mile home.

Villanelle

What is this chill that causes my unease,
crawls up my bent spine and makes me shiver,
hunched in prayer, forever on my knees?

It's not like the roar of a swarm of wild bees,
that drives maddened wolves to dive in the river –
what is this thrill that causes my unease?

It's not like the rush of wind in the trees-
that's too familiar to make my heart quiver,
bowed in prayer, forever on my knees.

It's not that I have some wasting disease,
that achingly pares down my life to a sliver –
What is this pang that causes my unease?

Has the great reckoning come, with licence to seize
and cast out my soul, were I not to deliver,
crouched in prayer, forever on my knees?

His compassion is such that I should not freeze,
were he to be present, the supreme life giver –
but in my stiff heart there still lives unease
huddled in prayer, forever on my knees.

Finding

Two buzzards loop above dark conifers,
A dog springs out to sample knee-deep pools;
The yellow acorns sign across rough heath
Past rocks, unrecognized, to sudden sights.

Not now the street-disturbed accustomed home,
But in a silent, starlit, night-dark room,
At once the restless sleep, as stress unwinds
Gives way, (Give thanks!) to unremembered dreams.

Here, marginal to neat, familiar life,
With mind and body seeking unknown states,
Respite from others' imposed urgencies
Releases thought-inspiring energy.

Minds clear, like mists, to show an avenue
Cut straight to freely chosen destiny.
The spaniel proved the quick-run, stone-bed stream;
Two buzzards loop above dark conifers.

Solanum Tuberosum

Shall I prepare you with a sprig of thyme
Beneath lamb roasting – taste should be a dream –
Or thinly sliced in pan with eggs and cream,
Or something *nouveau* – dill, basil and lime?
I could compose menus mind out of time –
Believe me, new Jerseys go well with bream –
From Beeton to Jamie recipes teem,
Is this the first song praising you in rhyme?
Yet carping critics are not far to seek,
For crisps, all salty, they say should be trashed
And there are problems with fat-sodden chips;
And though she may crave now for bubble'n'squeak,
A young girl's hopes of stardom may be dashed,
When she finds out that spuds put pounds on hips.

To the Jerusalem Artichoke
(Some Whimsy)

1. Misheard

What bend of mind self-mutilates and kills,
Yet leaves eternal icons –
The bandaged head, the rustic chair, and most of all
Those yellow – those spiralling sun flowers.

Follow the sun – a welcome command,
So to Umbrian plains the dutiful English go,
And in the heat of saffron tinted fields
Delight to hear melting roundly from the lips,
Girasole

– what did Shakespeare hear four centuries ago?
Could manuscript or mangled tongue do ought but
Render it Jerusalem?

– that mystic name that seeds
Quiet pilgrimage and blood crusade,
And still inspires the rugby forward, and the rural cook,
To join in unison and sing

2. The Song

Bring me my bowl and pastry cold,
Bring me my arrowroot entire;
Bring fresh mint here, not two hours old,
And set the pan upon the fire.

Last night I did the lentils soak,
And now I won't my spoon let drop,
Till I have served the artichoke
On bed of dhal with crusty top –

Jerusalem A-arti-ichoke!

My Box*

In my box is the strength I have lost,
the movement of the journeys I have made,
the enjoyment of relationships new and old.

My box is fashioned from clouds, white, gold and grey,
catching the sunlight before rain.

I will stand on my box to reach the future.

*First published in Still Life (United Press, 2004)

Mark Sayers

He drinks too much to be a Monk,
Wise women give him a wide berth.
A pen scribbles for all its worth,
Intent on flights of fantasy.
Kips on his bunk, now old and shrunk;
His dream? Poetic rampancy!

Déjà vu

There are those - who can make you feel
As if it's your first day at School
When you feel a fool, as a rule.
That look as if they can't conceal
The thought that you're an imbecile.
Subjecting one to ridicule,
Whilst managing to look so cool;
Why should one suffer this ordeal?

It matters not if it's The Club,
Or a pint in The Rose & Crown.
What matters is that you are new
And there's the rub; so they will snub
An embarrassed and awkward clown.
Déjà vu!... Could one misconstrue?

Stepping from Jane Austen's Pages

I wonder how you are, if you're
As quaint and pretty as you were
When we last met? No doubt you will
Have *that look* – so calm and tranquil
Which tends to make my old heart stir.
In purdah, you'd still have allure!

Stepping from Jane Austen's pages,
You can captivate in jeans.
If I could lose twenty five years,
Might I compete with all your peers
And, with luck, find I had the means
To sweep you off your feet – for ages?

Do you reveal a pensive air,
As if life is not all it seems?
I hope somewhere is your soul mate,
Someone who will appreciate
You as you are and in whose dreams,
Nightly you'll star – beyond compare!

The Book Club choice

Some weeks I share my home with some
Whom my instincts warn me to shun;
Why let these people now intrude
And linger, when they are so crude?

Why watch them as they fornicate,
Stagnate and seem so second rate,
As they pee on the earthen floor,
Disown their parents, furthermore?

Despised by mosquitoes who suck
Their blood; squashing, ... wiping the muck
In English never more mundane...
Where making love can cause pure pain,

Abortion raise its ugly head –
With 'amputated, ... emptied ... dead.'
Where some have no right to grow old:
So sordid and so uncontrolled.

When one's left wondering, 'Who?' and 'Why?'
And, 'Did her Father really die?'.
Where weeds have blood and throats constrict.
I wonder if we could have picked

A more repulsive glimpse of life,
Praised by 'the experts' who run rife,
Regarding this as so top notch,
As they reach down to scratch their crotch....

Thank God, this crew don't drawl and gall
In Maidenhead - but Montreal.
The Library can keep their book.
The monthly read? I'm off the hook!

'What Is the Hurry Anyway?'

I've seen you shuffling down the street
With worn tweed cap and unkempt hair,
Showing such signs of wear and tear,
Looking confused and somewhat numb.
You are alone and seldom meet
A friend; don't seem to have a chum.

You are subservient and meek
And sometimes wear a linen hat;
Can't eat much, ... none could call you fat
And your clothes have seen better days.
You've climbed in tandem up life's Peak
But now – are on your own, ... always.

Doreen died... which was a harsh blow:
The one who cooked and kept things clean
And now you haven't got a bean
To bless yourself with anyway.
Those hearth-glad days seem long ago,
Now life is dredged up with decay....

It's time to have your hearing aid
Checked... to make sure that it still works.
You never had a job with perks:
A car or an expense account.
You did as you were told, low-paid,
And were kicked out at the headcount.

They didn't care you'd been a Clerk
With the Firm... over thirty years.
Brand new and changing all the gears,
'We let go faces that don't fit'.
Cast in the dark, you lost your spark;
They didn't know or care one bit!

The feral youths noising next door,
Who taunt you as you're walking past,
Throw eggs at your windows and cast
Aspersions on your parents' ties; ...
You dare not raise your head, implore,
In case they give you two black eyes.

God bless you Old Boy... as you wait
At the bus-stop, looking resigned.
It's late, but you don't seem to mind;
'What is the hurry anyway?'....
Would that a soul mate made a date
To light up both your lives today!

Blessings from the Sky

Why should the rain make us feel sad?
That steady patter through the trees
Which brings moans from Troon to Torquay;
Not all have washing to put out.
Folk rejoice in Allahabad;
They know what rainfall's all about.

The blest monsoon for which they pray
To any Gods whom they may know,
'Please send rain so our crops can grow!'.
The plaintive *Brain Fever Bird's* cry
Is heard throughout the dusty day
Until blessings fall from the sky.

Bleak Winter's branches look so bare
And desolate as raindrops fall,
Yet they know, as in far Bengal,
How crucial is the Blessed Rain!
For they are also well aware
That their long roots will not complain.

Even the window panes look drear
As teardrops slowly trickle down.
The sky seems glum, tending to frown
Because the sun won't show his face
To bring us all a little cheer
In green Olde Englande, … our birthplace.

'What's the Party for?'

Friends who are partying, blest or heartsore,
Drinking and looking... or meeting a chum,
Why do you want to know, 'What is it for?'?

No, I'm not sailing off to Singapore
In search of cheongsams to whom I'll succumb, ...
Friends who are partying, blest or heartsore.

Hallowmass dark nights... and thoughts turn to War,
Lost love, fanatics and those left quite numb.
Why do you want to know, 'What is it for?'?

Weekly... I read of murders by the score
In Brixton, Basingstoke, Bristol or Brum, ...
Friends who are partying, blest or heartsore.

Young children kidnapped... causing an uproar;
A baby burnt to death; ... poor Dad and Mum!
Why do you want to know, 'What is it for?'?

Can it be two years since I closed the door,
Driving South feeling relieved... and yet glum?
Friends who are partying, blest or heartsore,
Why do you want to know, 'What is it for?'?

Rupert Hopkins

has   been writing poetry for as long as he can remember. He gets inspiration from his immediate world and from his own personal experience. He works in a Bristol City library.

Smiles and Cackles

Smiles and cackles in a witches' brew of
Misspoken squabbling syllables.

Hunched like a misshapen moulting broody hen
In the aisle of the deserted bus
Her battered umbrella paraded in the feathered straw yard
At full mast,
False sense of protection from the swift approaching storm cloud
Gathering
Unfurling and hurling into the beaten plough black cloud
equation.

Raises swords beaten like broken omelets into plough shares
Etch the rattled deep furrows drilled into her fertile ancient ghetto
brow,

Still blasted with sulphur smoke filled Warsaw uprising memories,
The bleak desecrated landscape sacrificed on the altar of tyranny
and destruction,
Flame throwers torching gutted building
Turning the once cosmopolitan and thriving city
Into a ghosted wasteland.

Heavy Hearted

Heavy hearted
Bowed down with weary downcast eyes
Her ancestors had choice ripped from the pores of their skin
Wrestled into blunt heavy handed chains.
Manacled like clusters of barnacles and hauled across bitter salt
tasting treacherous Atlantic crossing waves.
Exiled and banished into slavery.

And now
We exist
In twisted wombs
Spools of unprocessed film
Hung from gallows
In suspended animation.

Watch with halted breath as
Our life's dance and pirouette
In slow spider motion.

Float in a dream haze
Across silver gloss
Silent computer screen.

Wait in the process station
Halls filled with shadows of discontent
Kafkaesque novels transformed into
Grim reality.
Knocking bleakly at castle doors.
Receiving no reply before rough hands force one
To run through empty corridors of despair
Pursued by laughing manic pen wielding overseers.

Wait while personal papers and love letters and valentine cards are
sifted through and analyzed.
Financial statements examined brusquely with forensic combs and
scanning machines with microscopic vision
While politicians proclaim the dawning of the new frontiers of this
global market place where labour flows freely.

Wait in the flickering shadows of doubt and disbelief.
Remember our ancestors and blood brothers and sisters,
Wearily cutting and slicing sugar cane
Visions of freedom flow from the sugary sweet dripping sap

And still 202 years later
We are still forced to grovel and scrape one's forelock to the suited
Plantation over seer,
And now hanging onto silk threads and cord of long distant
Telephone conversation,
We dare to dream and wait for that hesitant call
Which allows us
To continue with our life.
Wait for that cell door to swing open on well-oiled hinge
For lovers' lips to smile and to roar
Like lions in the African savannah sunshine
And to embrace in the morning frosty flickering strip light
Of the bleak industrial airport terminal.

Mary Crowder

Mary has been creating poetry in the written, aural and visual arenas since 2006. Her exhibitions include The Heteronym Alphabet, A- Descending, READ; Dartington, Plymouth, Winchester, Colleges of Art, Reading Museum and RWA. She lives in Bristol, England with her goldfish Heathcliff.

Friendly Fire

Friendly fire
one blast
you're in the past.

Friendly fire
language of hell
a religious shell.

Friendly fire
political gain
no leader's in sighted frame.

Friendly fire
orders of hate
DEAD
you were
my mate.

A Family Fable

Rodney the rodent was running along
family provider, homemaker, inspiration to all
caught as the trap snapped, closed on its prey.
A white rat sacrifice,
the humans say.

Rowena, the daughter
screamed as she saw,
her father no longer able to tussle in fun.
For under the spring, his tail, mashed
cheese enticement, survival had dashed.

Rosalind, the mother, rodent supreme
cried as she witnessed
the treble unrelenting scene.
The sacrificial father, no longer a pretty pet,
as he tugged and gnawed at his death threat.

Richard, the son,
squeaked of unspeakable acts,
the white clan gathered, revengeful and haggard.
Preparing to riot, diseases to scatter, babies to bite
with no piper in sight to save the white slayer plight.

Sister and Student Nurse

Nurse Jones, stand straight,
your apron?
Hands scrubber up to the elbow. Good
follow me
hurry along.
Teaching all you students,
dear, dear.

Select the size,
now that's far too big,
you'll make Mr. Benson nervous.
Expiry date checked, appropriate needle selected, sterile swab,
Mr. Benson is in bed five.
Your hand's shaking, look professional.
Now Nurse Jones you must not fail,
carry the kidney dish with
confidence and knowing authority.

Well I Never Did

Well I never did,
never can't have
did has had.
Well I never.

Well I never did,
never can't have
did has had.
Did I ever
have never?

Well I never did,
never can't, did has,
did I?
Never!
Well well.

Charles Thompson

writes about people he knows; he also writes on themes that arise from his contemplation of Nature.

What Cracked Hope of God or Knowledge

What cracked hope of God or knowledge
Under the mountains where the houses tumble?

I would say more
But I know nothing of this

My father – his memory loosening –
Smiles so genially –
Temper mostly gone.

May has put forth
Her royal weeds and flowers.

I would my father's dear head
Be crowned with these

My son chucks sticks to the river
Checking their speed.

Things I say
Around this green season.

I Woke That Sleeping Day

I woke that sleeping day to find again
I knew nothing – only an aching heart

And dream-like thoughts that led me
To the green ones who are my friends;

And how they yearn and how the poetry
Flows from their yearning

One yearns for lost poets – great ones –
Their keening call spells now.

Another has compassion; he laments lost souls
Whose feast of life is thrown down.

Another pitches a joke a sonnet or an opinion
Jauntily in a pub's upper room.

Friends – my sleeping heart.

My Father Sleeps Through August

My father sleeps through August
It is the long sleep of age

And my brother frets
His art calls him
And his gardens
Yet he has to stay
With the old man

Organize meals, drugs, carers, sleep

'I'm just going to take a week off –
 have a holiday in France –'

'I love him in small doses' he says.

I Forgot You, Frog

I forgot you, frog,
        as I pored over Coleridge
                and his dusty high road of custom

I forgot how I met you and how
        your blotched eyes stared blindly from
                a patch of mud, enclosed
                        by the rain-circled grass

I forgot you at the evening service where
        films and slides exhorted me
                to 'preserve the environment'
                        and – to be thankful.

I forgot you, in your August
Tense trance of being as you waited
Some electricity to touch you – static!

                Unseen, in the night-frost,
                This October, I forgot you!

                 I forgot your fierce electric leap

                – your rhythmic leap!

                How you suddenly split the air

                And with a nudge of the grasses
                – and a shuffle

                – gone where nettles kept you secret.

        Amid the wettened grass clump – by the water-butt

        secret!

I remember now your beating pulse –
Moving as you did not move – so unafraid
Like a pulse of water.

Now you order yourself differently in my imagination.

Raindrops Like Heavy Bubbles Fall

Raindrops like heavy bubbles fall in South America;
Lightning shrieks into the wind.

My father said 'Don't weep!'
'You were a Headmaster.' I said 'Remember!'

His legs were like dry sticks, shuffling to the loo,
The clocks had turned back the night before.

'And was Uncle Egbert a teacher?
The neat calm room. 'Creature?'

'Where did he live?' 'Yorkshire'
The nurse brings in supper.

'Au revoir mon père' I said
'Au revoir with a mute e eh!
Au revoir mon fils.'

I passed the sandstone church;
Glass stained with reds, yellows, purples;
The soft humming of a hymn.'

'We'll put a rustle mat in his room,'
Said my mother 'so we know if he falls.'

And so she ate her soup and a cracker.

'Every morning the Baptist lady visits –
Makes me a cup of tea. Thank you
For the lovely chocolate.'

Lightning speared itself onto the church roof
Rain smashed into the lanes like monsoons.

Olga Amelina Unwin

Olga is a Russian-born Bristolian who was primarily brought up and educated in Bristol but also spent many years living on-and-off in Berlin, where she was part of the CWG (Creative Writing Group), a group of international writers, with whom she was published last year with her poem ' The Postbox.' She has been writing poetry since her early teenage years and has recently moved into short and childrens' fiction. She is also an artist, specialising in fine illustration and her other hobbies include music and movies. She is delighted to be back in her childhood town, although she does sometimes miss the charms of Berlin.

Bristol Artists

They were the gorge-dwellers;
introverts yearning out yet keeping in,
saturated with doubt and longing for the beyond,
brought to them by the southern wind.

Among Georgian facades and cliffs they hid their stark
seeming of existence, clothed in the waving leaves of trees,
a harbour crane's harsh swingings to the spirits of older times,
conversing with the pirate shadows on hearing summer

heat on Blackboy Hill. Among the Broadmead tracksuits,
city centre slums, among the hoodies skateboarding
over hopes and dreams, they stirred themselves
beyond their means and glorified the town to the newcomer.

Stralsund

A beach stage stood there, advertising 'Westside Story' –
America was forcing itself upon the Baltic waves.

We saw Maria in a simple dress, memorising
'Tonight' in gruff, strained wording;

a Grettel impostor, golden locks neatly dyed
to look Hispanic – history on the rebound.

The sailing boats beyond the Arrow[1]
carried no cargo; no amber, resin or wax,

trading only in white-clad, manicured vamps,
leaning on over-tanned playboys, cool and dour.

Just then, a girl passed by, her mother saying,
'And in 1628, during the Thirty Years War,[2]

Stralsund made the Emperor withdraw.'
That night, when we went to take the train,

I thought I saw a merchant on the empty shore,
the Lübeck Law[3] granted to this No Man's Land once more.

1: 'Strale/ow' or 'Arrow' was the original name of the site of the initial
settlement of Stralsund (then a fishing village) in pre-mediaeval ages
and till 1240 when Prince Winzlaw I of Rügen, on granting it extra land,
finally called it ' Stralesund.'

2: The Holy Roman Emperor Ferdinand II (1578-1637) was one in a long line of
Germanic kings who continued the title of Emperor as first claimed by Charlemagne
in c. 799. The Thirty Years War (1618–1648) was largely a conflict between
Protestants and Catholics across Germany but involved most of the countries of
Europe. Stralsund, a Hanseatic port town vital for trade and defence, was a target
and in 1628 it was invaded by Ferdinand II's troops. The Battle of Stralsund started in
May 1628 and ended in August when Stralsund was successfully defended by it's
allegiance of Swedes, Scots and the town's inhabitants.

3: The Lübeck Law still serves as the foundation for many German town laws and
granted a city independence from it's surroundings and from autocratic rule by a tribal
monarchs or regional dukes and kings. Prince Winzlaw I of Rügen granted it to
Stralsund in 1234.